Some Days You Really Need
a Good Quote

Collected by Walter Shawlee 2

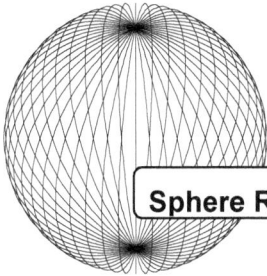

Sphere Research Corporation

Collection and Contents Copyright: 1999, 2010
by
Sphere Research Corporation

ISBN:
978-0-557-36015-4

I love a good quote, especially one that not only captures an idea fully and clearly, but also comes from a mind you respect. Sometimes the strange combination of those two things is a huge surprise. They are like very short stories that suddenly explain something that has been troubling you for a long time.

Every so often, they take your breath away, because the idea is so strong, and has somehow reached right into your heart through so many years of human history. It can be astonishing to read Thomas Jefferson or Albert Einstein and see that they thought about the very same issues you do today.

I have been collecting them for so many years, I have lost track. These come from every possible source, literally spanning thousands of years. They are checked where possible, but even if these should be flawed as they appear, they remain a delight to read.

Just for convenience, these are mainly in alphabetical order by the author, but since that isn't always ideal, the extra end section with some favorites is just in the order I happen to like.

The best effect of any book is that it
excites the reader to self activity
Thomas Carlyle

Growth for the sake of growth is the ideology of the cancer cell.
Edward Abbey

The future comes one day at a time
Dean Acheson

It is easier to fight for one's principles than to live up to them.
Alfred Adler

If at first you don't succeed, you're running about average.
M.H. Alderson

I have not seen any problem, however complicated, which when you looked at it in the right way, did not become still more complicated.
Paul Anderson

The worst form of inequality is to make
unequal things equal.
Aristotle

The saddest aspect of life right now
is that science gathers knowledge
faster than society gathers wisdom.
Isaac Asimov

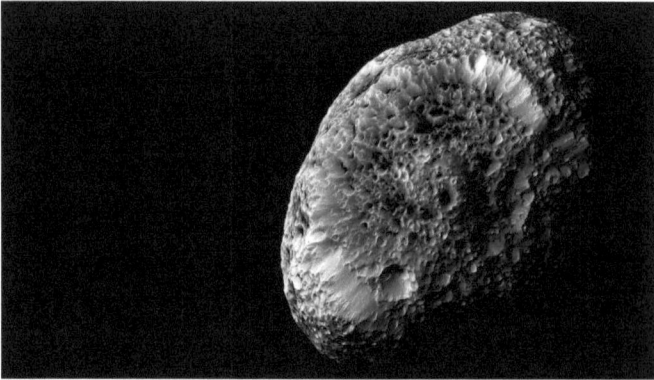

Man prefers to believe what he prefers
to be true.
Francis Bacon

War would end if the dead could return.
Stanley Baldwin

Money is a terrible master, but an
excellent servant.
P.T. Barnum

Nothing is really work
unless you would rather be doing
something else.
James M. Barrie

Every man has a right to his opinion,
but no man has a right to be wrong with
his facts.
Bernard Baruch

Art is I, science is we.
Claude Bernard

You can see a lot by observing.
Yogi Berra

A man who stands for nothing
will fall for anything.
W.A.C. Bennett

Wise men learn by other men's mistakes,
fools by their own.
H.G. Bohn

Ours is a world of nuclear giants and ethical infants.
We know more about war than we know about
peace, more about killing than we know about
living.
Omar N. Bradley

Crime is contagious. If the government
becomes a lawbreaker,
it breeds contempt for the law.
Justice Louis D. Brandeis

Goodwill towards all is true religion
Buddhacarita (The Acts of the Buddha)

Genius does what it must; talent does
what it can.
Edward Bulwer-Lytton

The only thing necessary for the triumph of evil
is for good men to do nothing.
Edmund Burke

The best effect of any book is that it
excites the reader to self activity
Thomas Carlyle

I do not believe in the collective wisdom
of individual ignorance.
Thomas Carlyle

Man is what he believes.
Anton Chekhov

The most common commodity in this country
is unrealized potential.
Calvin Coolidge

The best argument against democracy
is a five-minute conversation with the average
voter.
Winston Churchill

As always, victory finds a hundred fathers,
but defeat is an orphan.
Count Ciano

A faith that cannot survive collision with
the truth is not worth many regrets.
Arthur C. Clarke

The tendencies of democracies are, in all
things, to mediocrity, since the tastes,
knowledge, and principles of the majority
form the tribunal of appeal.
James Fennimore Cooper

Fraud and falsehood dread examination.
Truth invites it.
Thomas Cooper

The belief in a supernatural source of evil is not
necessary;
men alone are quite capable of every wickedness.
Joseph Conrad

Nothing in life is to be feared. It is only to
be understood.
Marie Curie

The hottest places in hell are reserved for those who in times of great moral crisis maintained their neutrality.
Dante

He who allows oppression shares the crime.
Erasmus Darwin

We are here to make another world.
W. Edwards Deming

Improve constantly and forever every process for planning, production and service.
W. Edwards Deming

Nothing is so easy as to deceive one's self; for what we wish, we readily believe.
Demosthenes (350BC)

A state is better governed if it has but few laws, and those laws strictly enforced.
Rene Descarte

Those in power want only to perpetuate it.
William O. Douglas

Nor is the people's judgment always true;
The most may err as grossly as the few.
John Dryden

The most beautiful thing we can
experience is the mysterious.
He to whom this emotion is a stranger,
who can no longer wonder and stand
rapt in awe is as good as dead;
his eyes are closed.
Albert Einstein

Perfection of means and confusion of
ends seems to characterize our age.
Albert Einstein

No man thoroughly understands a truth
until he has contended against it.
Ralph Waldo Emerson

Regulation is the substitution of error for chance.
Fred Emery

How you measure the performance
of your managers
directly affects the way they act.
Gustave Flaubert

It is not the employer who pays the
wages---he only handles the money.
It is the product that pays the wages.
Henry Ford

Creative minds have always been known
to survive any kind of bad training.
Anna Freud

When I am working on a problem, I never
think about beauty. I think only of how to
solve the problem. But when I have
finished, if the solution is not beautiful, I
know it is wrong.
Buckminster Fuller

The service we render others is really the
rent we pay for our room on Earth.
Sir Wilfred Grenfell

You miss 100% of the shots you never take.
Wayne Gretzky

Many of the insights of a saint stem from
his experience as a sinner.
Eric Hoffer

Nothing in the world, not all the armies, is
so powerful as an idea whose time has come.
Victor Hugo

Facts do not cease to exist because they
are ignored.
Aldous Huxley

In nature there are neither rewards or
punishments; there are only
consequences.
George Iles

I'm a great believer in luck and I find the
harder I work the more I have of it.
Thomas Jefferson

The natural progress of things is for liberty
to yield and government to gain ground.
Thomas Jefferson

The road to hell is paved with good
intentions.
Samuel Johnson

Love doesn't make the world go around,
love is what makes the ride worthwhile.
Franklin P. Jones

Experience is what enables you to
recognize a mistake when you make it
again.
Franklin P. Jones

Our task is not to fix the blame for the
past, but to fix the course for the future.
John F. Kennedy

There is no calamity greater than lavish desires.
There is no greater guilt than discontentment.
And there is no greater disaster than greed.
Lao-tzu

It may be those who do most,
dream most.
Stephen Leacock

Tact is the ability to describe others as
they see themselves.
Abraham Lincoln

No man is good enough to govern another man
without that other's consent.
Abraham Lincoln

Those who suppress freedom always do so in the name of law and order.
John Lindsay

Corrupt, stupid grasping functionaries will make at least as big a muddle of socialism as stupid, grasping and acquisitive employers can make of capitalism.
Walter Lippmann

Truth in science can be defined as the working hypothesis best suited to open the way to the next better one.
Konrad Lorenz

An individual has not started living until he can rise above the narrow confines of his individualistic concerns to the broader concerns of humanity.
Martin Luther King Jr.

We are prone to judge success by the index of our salaries or the size of our automobiles, rather than by the quality of our service and relationship to humanity.
Martin Luther King Jr.

The road to affluence is paved with good inventions.
Charles J.C. Lyall

Knowledge consists not of facts themselves but the understanding of the relationships among facts.
Charles J.C. Lyall

Decide promptly, but never give any reasons.
Your decisions may be right,
but your reasons are sure to be wrong.
Lord Mansfield

People with bad consciences
always fear the judgment of children.
Mary McCarthy

Lord, grant that I may always desire more
than I can accomplish
Michelangelo

The greatest danger of bombs is in
the explosion of stupidity that they provoke.
Octave Mirabeau

If you steal from one, it's plagiarism; if you steal from many, it's research.
Wilson Mizner

Trend is not destiny.
Lewis Mumford

Our major obligation is not to mistake slogans for solutions.
Edward Morrow

If liberty means anything at all, it means the right to tell people what they do not want to hear.
George Orwell

An evil life is a kind of death.
Ovid

Men never do evil so completely and cheerfully
as when they do it from religious conviction.
Blaise Pascal

Chance favors the trained mind.
Louis Pasteur

What is honored in a country will be
cultivated there.
Plato

Concentrated power has always been the
enemy of liberty.
Ronald Reagan

If you are afraid of being lonely, don't try
to be right.
Jules Renard

Even if you're on the right track, you'll get
run over if you just sit there.
Will Rogers

No one can make you feel inferior without
your consent.
Eleanor Roosevelt

Do what you can,
with what you have,
where you are.
Theodore Roosevelt

In order that people may be happy in their work,
these three things are needed:
They must be fit for it.
They must not do too much of it.
And they must have a sense of success in it.
John Ruskin

There is hardly anything in the world
that some man cannot make a little worse
and sell a little cheaper.
John Ruskin

One's friends are that part of the human
race with which one can be human.
George Santayana

Those who cannot remember the past
are condemned to repeat it.
George Santayana

Liberty means responsibility. That is why
most men dread it.
George Bernard Shaw

God is not finished yet.
Walter Shawlee 2

Appearance overpowers even the truth.
Simonides of Ceos

Poverty is no disgrace to a man, but is
profoundly inconvenient.
Rev. Sydney Smith

There are few sorrows, however poignant,
in which a good income is of no avail.
Logan Pearsall Smith

The unexamined life is not worth living.
Socrates

All warfare is based on deception.
Sun Tzu

A man should never be ashamed to own
he has been in the wrong,
which is but saying, in other words,
that he is wiser today than he was yesterday.
Jonathan Swift

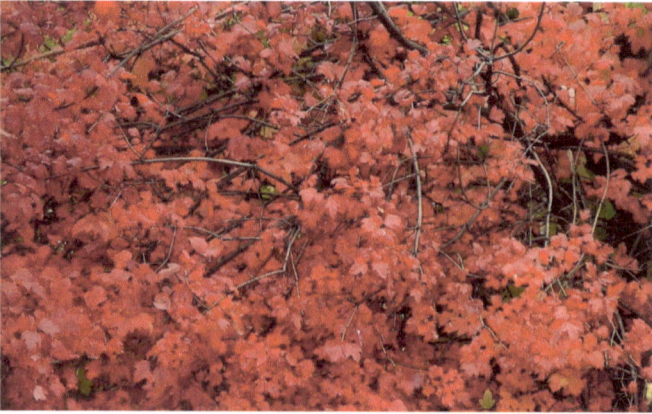

The more corrupt the state, the more numerous the laws.
Tacitus

Men have become the tools of their tools.
Henry David Thoreau

If you can't convince them, confuse them.
Harry S. Truman

Money won't buy happiness, but it will pay the salaries of a large research staff to study the problem.
Bill Vaughan

As long as people believe in absurdities, they will commit atrocities.
Voltaire

It is dangerous to be right
in matters on which the established authorities
are wrong.
Voltaire

Nature tends toward equilibrium.
Mel Webster

Be obscure clearly.
E.B. White

The best career advice to give to the young is
"Find out what you like doing best
and get someone to pay you for doing it."
Katharine Whitehorn

Only the shallow know themselves.
Oscar Wilde

You are who you are, regardless of who
you think you are.
Oscar Wilde

A great deal of formal ethics
is clever evasion.
Ludwig Wittgenstein

All empty souls tend toward extreme
opinions.
William Butler Yeats

Some people handle the truth carelessly.
Others never touch it at all.
Unknown attribution

No single snowflake ever feels responsible
for the avalanche.
Unknown attribution

**These have particular significance for me,
so I hope you enjoy them as much as I do.**

I tremble for my country when I reflect
that God is just.
Thomas Jefferson

A doctor can bury his mistakes, but an
architect can only advise his client to
plant vines.
Frank Lloyd Wright

It wasn't raining when Noah built the ark.
Howard Ruff

Faced with the choice between changing
one's mind, and proving that there is no
need to do so, almost everybody gets
busy on the proof.
John Kenneth Galbraith

The promised land always looks better
from a distance.
Pat Healy

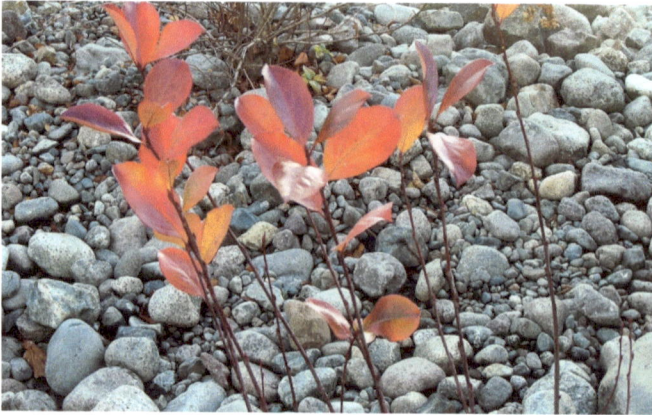

No matter what you believe, you always
find some people on your side that you
wish were on the other side.
Jascha Heifetz

When we all think alike,
no one thinks very much.
Walter Lippmann

After all is said and done, a hell of a lot
more is said than done.
Clark Olmstead

A good reputation is more valuable than money.
Publilius Syrus   Maxim 108

There is more to life than increasing its
speed.
Mohandas K. Gandhi

A president cannot always be popular.
Harry S. Truman

Criticize behavior, not people.
Paul Rubin

Customers want 1/4" holes, not 1/4" drills.
MBA Magazine

Example is leadership.
Albert Schweitzer

Life is hard; it's harder if you're stupid.
John Wayne

All progress depends
on the unreasonable man.
George Bernard Shaw

Quality is what the customer says he
needs, not what our tests indicate is
satisfactory.
Tom Peters

Nowadays people know the price of everything
and the value of nothing.
Oscar Wilde

Nobody is too old to learn,
but a lot of people keep putting it off.
William O'Neill

Our problems cannot be solved
by the same level of thinking that created them.
Albert Einstein

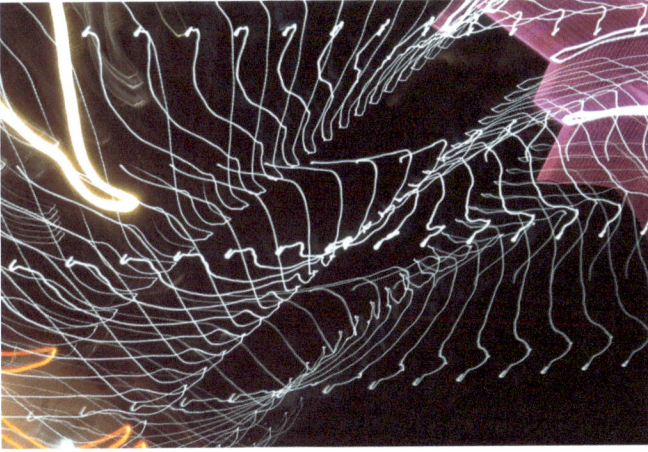

The trouble with doing something
right the first time
is that nobody appreciates
how difficult it was.
Walt West

The road to hell is paved
with good excuses.
Walter Shawlee 2

The most exciting phrase to hear in science,
the one that heralds new discoveries,
is not 'Eureka!' but 'That's funny...'
Isaac Asimov

Much more is known than is actually true.
J. R. Pierce   ('50s and '60s Bell Labs worker)

One, with God, is always a majority,
but many a martyr has been burned at the stake
while the votes were being counted.
Thomas B. Reed

It is not enough to do your best;
you must know what to do,
and then do your best.
W. Edwards Deming

He who does not punish evil
Commands it to be done.
Leonardo Da Vinci

This short intellectual coffee break is
brought to you by the interesting people at
SPHERE RESEARCH CORPORATION,
who just happen to collect quotes, and who also
believe the following to be true:

"Letting a powerful idea
loose in the world is like
letting light into a darkened
room. It remains
unchanged, but it looks
completely different."

www.ingramcontent.com/pod-product-compliance
Lightning Source LLC
Chambersburg PA
CBHW041228270326
41935CB00002B/12